0104977

BASEBALL LEGENDS

Hank Aaron
Grover Cleveland Alexander
Ernie Banks
Johnny Bench
Yogi Berra
Roy Campanella
Roberto Clemente
Ty Cobb
Dizzy Dean
Joe DiMaggio
Bob Feller
Jimmie Foxx
Lou Gehrig
Bob Gibson
Rogers Hornsby
Walter Johnson
Sandy Koufax
Mickey Mantle
Christy Mathewson
Willie Mays
Stan Musial
Satchel Paige
Brooks Robinson
Frank Robinson
Jackie Robinson
Babe Ruth
Tom Seaver
Duke Snider
Warren Spahn
Willie Stargell
Honus Wagner
Ted Williams
Carl Yastrzemski
Cy Young

CHELSEA HOUSE PUBLISHERS

HONUS WAGNER

Jack Kavanagh

Introduction by
Jim Murray

Senior Consultant
Earl Weaver

CHELSEA HOUSE PUBLISHERS
New York • Philadelphia

CHELSEA HOUSE PUBLISHERS
Editorial Director: Richard Rennert
Executive Managing Editor: Karyn Gullen Browne
Executive Editor: Scan Dolan
Copy Chief: Robin James
Picture Editor: Adrian G. Allen
Art Director: Robert Mitchell
Manufacturing Director: Gerald Levine
Production Coordinator: Marie Claire Cebrián-Ume

Baseball Legends
Senior Editor: Philip Koslow

Staff for HONUS WAGNER
Associate Editor: David Carter
Editorial Assistant: Kelsey Goss
Designer: Cambraia Magalhães
Picture Researcher: Alan Gottlieb
Cover Illustration: Daniel O'Leary

First Printing

1   3   5   7   9   8   6   4   2

Library of Congress Cataloging-in-Publication Data

Kavanagh, Jack
Honus Wagner / Jack Kavanagh; introd. by Jim Murray.
p. cm.—(Baseball legends)
Includes bibliographical references and index.
Summary: A biography of the Pittsburgh Pirates shortstop who was one of the greatest hitters and
fielders in baseball history.
ISBN 0-7910-1193-3
ISBN 0-7910-1227-1 (pbk.)
1. Wagner, Honus—Juvenile literature. 2. Baseball players—United States—Biography—Juvenile lit-
erature. 3. Pittsburgh Pirates (Baseball team)—History—Juvenile literature. [1. Wagner, Honus. 2.
Baseball players.] I. Title. II. Series.
GV865.W33K38 1992   9-128898
796.357'092—dc20   CIP
[B]   AC

5/2001
Superior
$16.95

CONTENTS

WHAT MAKES A STAR

Jim Murray

No one has ever been able to explain to me the mysterious alchemy that makes one man a .350 hitter and another player, more or less identical in physical makeup, hard put to hit .200. You look at an Al Kaline, who played with the Detroit Tigers from 1953 to 1974. He was pale, stringy, almost poetic-looking. He always seemed to be struggling against a bad case of mononucleosis. But with a bat in his hands, he was King Kong. During his career, he hit 399 home runs, rapped out 3,007 hits, and compiled a .297 batting average.

Form isn't the reason. The first time anybody saw Roberto Clemente step into the batter's box for the Pittsburgh Pirates, the best guess was that Clemente would be back in Double A ball in a week. He had one foot in the bucket and held his bat at an awkward angle—he looked as though he couldn't hit an outside pitch. A lot of other ballplayers may have had a better-looking stance. Yet they never led the National League in hitting in four different years, the way Clemente did.

Not every ballplayer is born with the ability to hit a curveball. Nor is exceptional hand-eye coordination the key to heavy hitting. Big-league locker rooms are filled with players who have all the attributes, save one: discipline. Every baseball man can tell you a story about a pitcher who throws a ball faster than anyone has ever seen but who has no control on or *off* the field.

The Hall of Fame is full of people who transformed themselves into great ballplayers by working at the sport, by studying the game, and making sacrifices. They're overachievers—and winners. If you want to find them, just watch the World Series. Or simply read about New York Yankee great Lou Gehrig; Ted Williams, "the Splendid Splinter" of the Boston Red Sox; or the Dodgers' strikeout king Sandy Koufax.

A pitcher *should* be able to win a lot of ballgames with a 98-miles-per-hour fastball. But what about the pitcher who wins 20 games a year with a fastball so slow that you can catch it with your teeth? Bob Feller of the Cleveland Indians got into the Hall of Fame with a blazing fastball that glowed in the dark. National League star Grover Cleveland Alexander got there with a pitch that took considerably longer to reach the plate; but when it did arrive, the pitch was exactly where Alexander wanted it to be—and the last place the batter expected it to be.

There are probably more players with exceptional ability who didn't make it to the major leagues than there are who did. A number of great hitters, bored with fielding practice, had to be dropped from their team because their home-run production didn't make up for their lapses in the field. And then there are players like Brooks Robinson of the Baltimore Orioles, who made himself into a human vacuum cleaner at third base because he knew that working hard to become an expert fielder would win him a job in the big leagues.

A star is not something that flashes through the sky. That's a comet. Or a meteor. A star is something you can steer ships by. It stays in place and gives off a steady glow; it is fixed, permanent. A star works at being a star.

And that's how you tell a star in baseball. He shows up night after night and takes pride in how brightly he shines. He's Willie Mays running so hard his hat keeps falling off; Ty Cobb sliding to stretch a single into a double; Lou Gehrig, after being fooled in his first two at-bats, belting the next pitch off the light tower because he's taken the time to study the pitcher. Stars never take themselves for granted. That's why they're stars.

1

COLLISION COURSE FOR TWO TITANS

"Hey, Krauthead—I'm coming down on the next pitch." Ty Cobb snarled his challenge to Honus Wagner in the 1909 World Series.

"I'll be waiting," the Pittsburgh shortstop replied to Detroit's great hitter, but so softly that only Dots Miller, the Pirates second baseman, heard him. In the newspapers, Honus Wagner was nicknamed the Flying Dutchman, and Ty Cobb was the Georgia Peach. But down on the ballfield, they called each other by harsher names.

Cobb's skills as a hitter and base stealer depended a great deal on intimidation. A well-muscled six feet one, Cobb would fight anyone, anywhere. Wagner, two inches shorter but packing 200 pounds on his barrel-shaped frame, was equally impressive; yet he never fought anyone. It was not his way to start fights—the good-natured Dutchman tried to stay out of them.

Wagner was not about to back down from Cobb's challenge, however. Not with a world championship at stake. As Cobb bore down on second base, Wagner swiftly moved to cover the

Two of the greatest baseball players of all time, Honus Wagner and Ty Cobb, compare bats before their epic confrontation in the 1909 World Series. Cobb, known for his aggressive playing style, said of Wagner, "[He] is the only man I can't scare."

bag. Pirates catcher George Gibson fired a perfect throw, right above the base and well ahead of the speeding Cobb. In one motion, Wagner speared the ball, sidestepped Cobb's flashing spikes, and tagged his rival square in the face, opening a gash in Cobb's lip that required three stitches. Yet the umpire, Silk O'Loughlin, flung his arms out, palms down, and bellowed, "Safe!" By going for Cobb's head, Wagner had allowed the Detroit star to get his foot on the bag before the tag was applied. Cobb had stolen second—but Wagner had made him pay a price.

Cobb was the premier base stealer of his time, and in 1909 he had led everyone with 71 stolen bases. But never again would he try to steal second against the Pirates. Not with Wagner waiting there. In fact, except for a daring steal of home in the next game, Cobb did not steal another base in the Series. Meanwhile, Wagner, who had led his league in stolen bases five times, set two World Series records for stolen bases in 1909. He stole a total of six, and this record stood 58 years until Lou Brock broke it (with seven) in 1967. Even more impressive were Wagner's three stolen bases in one inning of Game 3, a record that may well last forever.

But Wagner and Cobb were more than just base stealers—much more. Each had been his league's batting champ in 1909. Cobb, who was appearing in his third straight World Series with Detroit, had just wrapped up a Triple Crown year with a .377 average, 167 RBIs, and 9 home runs. He was also first in hits, runs, and slugging average. Wagner, at 35, was 12 years older than Cobb. Still, he had led the National League in batting with a .339 average and in RBIs (100), as well as in slugging average and doubles.

*Wagner rounds first base after stroking a base hit during the 1909 season.
Despite his bowlegs and burly 200-pound frame, Wagner was a standout
baserunner who led the league in stolen bases five times.*

FORCE THE TRAINER   LEACH   BYRNE   HOWARD CAMNITZ   O'CONNOR   BRANDON   LEEVER   ABBATICCHIO   HYATT   MADDOX   WILSON   ABSTEIN   LEIFIELD

With these two superstars leading their teams, the 1909 World Series became one of the most hard fought ever played. (Ten batters were hit by pitches, Wagner being plunked twice and Cobb once. The competition was so fierce that it took four umpires instead of the customary two to keep the Series under control.) After the Pirates won the opener, the series seesawed until the climactic seventh game in Detroit. Wagner later called it his greatest game, although credit for the 8–0 win was given mostly to the Pittsburgh pitcher, Babe Adams. A rookie who had started only 12 games during the season, Adams had been a surprise choice to open the World Series. After winning Game 1, he notched another victory in Game 5. And then, with only two days' rest, he was chosen to pitch the deciding game.

Fred Clarke, Pittsburgh's player-manager, also starred in Game 7, hitting two home runs, a World Series record at the time. But even though Wagner contributed only one hit to the Pirates clincher, it was a big one. With two runners on

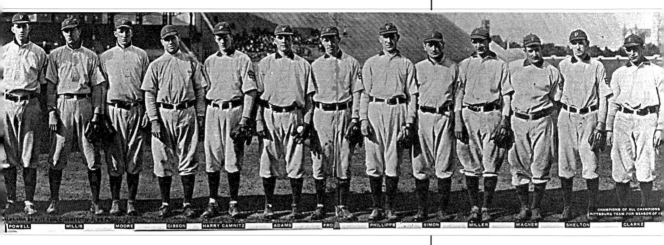

POWELL   WILLIS   MOORE   GIBSON   HARRY CAMNITZ   ADAMS   FRO   PHILLIPPE   SIMON   MILLER   WAGNER   SHELTON   CLARKE

base in the sixth inning, he hit a long double that raised the score from 4–0 to 6–0, an almost insurmountable margin in an era when home runs were scarce.

When the last out was made, the Pirates had beaten the Tigers for the World Championship, and Honus Wagner had outhit Ty Cobb by more than 100 percentage points, .333 to .231. The 1909 confrontation between two of baseball's greatest players had been much heralded, and it turned out to be the only time in their long careers that the two legends would ever meet on the ballfield.

The final game of the World Series had been played in Detroit. As soon as it was over, the players scattered to their off-season homes. Honus Wagner went happily back to a jubilant Pittsburgh, where he had lived all his life. If ever there was a "hometown hero," it was Honus Wagner in 1909.

A team photo of the 1909 Pittsburgh Pirates, taken after their World Series victory over the Detroit Tigers. Wagner considered the Series finale, in which the Pirates blanked the Tigers by an 8–0 margin, his greatest game.

2
YOUNG HONUS

Johannes Peter Wagner was born in Mansfield (now Carnegie), Pennsylvania, on February 24, 1874. The National League, where he would play for 21 seasons and coach for 18 more, did not yet exist. Wagner's father, Peter, was an immigrant from Bavaria in southern Germany. Peter Wagner and his wife, Catherine, settled in western Pennsylvania, where they raised five sons and a daughter. The region was home to many other German immigrants, whose nationality, in their native language, was *Deutsch*. Most English speakers found it easier to say "Dutch," and for this reason Wagner was later known as the Flying Dutchman. As a child, Johannes was affectionately called Hans or Honus, the German equivalent of Johnny.

Coal mining was a major industry in western Pennsylvania, and the five Wagner brothers fol-

Pennsylvania coal miners, photographed in 1909. At the age of 12, Honus Wagner left school to join his father and brothers in the mines of western Pennsylvania, but his baseball talent eventually proved the ticket to a better life.

lowed their father into the mines as soon as they were old enough. Hans, the baby of the family, quit school at the age of 12 to take his turn. "It was spring when I went to the mines to work and I was given what they called 'a boy's car,' " Wagner later recalled. "We needed the money and I loaded two tons of coal a day at 79 cents a ton, a boy's pay."

Two years later, Honus took over a man's role, swinging a pickax deep in the earth. He was small then and could squeeze into places that bigger men could not. During the next five years, he rarely saw daylight during the winter months. Along with his father and brothers, he would go into the mines before dawn and come out after sunset.

Only on Sundays could Honus and his friends play baseball in a vacant lot near the Wagners' house in Mansfield, just outside the sprawling city of Pittsburgh. The streets of Mansfield were unpaved and lit with gas lamps. The coal the miners dug from the earth was shoveled into the furnaces of the steel and iron mills, and the skies were dark with fumes pouring out of the city's smokestacks. Still, the boys could always find a baseball diamond on which to play, and all five Wagner brothers were in love with the game. At one point they even had their own team. "That's how I came to be pretty good in all positions," Wagner later explained. "On our family team, you had to learn how to play everywhere, as we were always shifting."

Honus was the star of a team of 12-year-olds, the Oregons. From the start he was a fierce competitor. One day, the story goes, Honus came to bat in the ninth inning with two outs and the Oregons trailing by a single run. The tying run was on base, and a home run would win the game. Honus belted the ball deep into the outfield: it got past the fielders, and the speedy Honus was a sure bet to circle the bases. Unfortunately, the boy already on base was the slowest runner on the team. Honus knew that if he passed the other boy, he would be called out. But if he waited for his teammate to reach the plate, they would both be tagged.

As far as Honus could tell, there was only one thing to do: he picked up the slower boy and carried him the rest of the way. Honus deposited the runner on the brick being used for home plate, then touched it himself a split second before the catcher could tag him. That the boys had bet five dollars on the game—55 cents of it belonged to Honus—may have had something to do with that herculean effort, but the youngster's pure drive and energy were typical of how he would play ball in the future.

By the time he was 16, Wagner had joined his hometown Mansfield team in the semiprofessional Allegheny League. He played any position that needed to be played, usually shortstop or the outfield. When there was a catcher strong enough to handle his fastball, Honus would pitch as well. "I had a fast ball, but not much control," Wagner later admitted. "It's one thing to make a throw across the diamond that a first baseman can reach, but it is another matter to get the ball over the plate from the pitcher's mound."

Nevertheless, it was as a pitcher that Wagner got his first chance in organized baseball. Al Wagner, who was already a professional player with Steubenville, launched an all-out campaign to convince his manager to take a look at his kid

Wagner (back row, third from left) played for the Atlantic League's Paterson, New Jersey, team in 1896. After batting .349 and .379 in his two years with Paterson, Wagner attracted the attention of major league scouts—in 1898, the Louisville Colonels purchased his contract for $2,100.

brother Honus. "I'll give the boy a tryout," the Steubenville manager finally said, "but he has to be here this afternoon at two o'clock." That was a lot easier said than done. In 1895 there was no telephone at the Wagner house, 50 miles away, so Al sent Honus a telegram: "Got you a job as pitcher. Be here by two o'clock sure."

The only way to get to Steubenville was by train, and the next passenger train was not scheduled to arrive in Steubenville until after two o'clock. But that did not stop Wagner. He hopped a freight train and showed up just in the nick of time. In all the rush, though, he had come as he was. No uniform, no glove, and worst of all, no baseball spikes.

The uniform and glove were no problem—Wagner could borrow those. But the spikes were another matter altogether because the youngster had huge feet. He finally squeezed them into a pair of his brother's baseball shoes, but in only 15 minutes he split them open and had to cast them aside. Then, bareheaded and barefoot, he stood on the mound and showed the manager a fastball that won him a place on the team.

The Steubenville squad provided their new recruit with the right size shoes by simply ordering them from Pittsburgh. But what Steubenville could not find was a catcher who could handle Wagner's fastballs. And so he became the team's shortstop. Before the 1895 season ended, Wagner had batted .402 in 44 games for Steubenville; .365 in 20 games for Adrian in the Michigan State League, and .369 in 65 games for Warren in the Iron-Oil League. Word about the hard-hitting youngster spread, and Ed Barrow heard the news. Barrow, a future member of the Baseball Hall of Fame, was then managing the Atlantic League's Paterson, New Jersey, team, and he signed Wagner for the 1896 season.

Playing mostly in the outfield, Wagner batted .349 his first season with Paterson and was hitting .379 the next year when he was approached by Harry Pulliam, president of the 12-team National League. Pulliam had been scouting the Atlantic League for players, and none impressed him as much as Wagner. After signing his first major league contract, Wagner was assigned to the National League's team in Louisville, Kentucky.

On July 19, 1897, the nervous rookie made his major league debut against the Baltimore Orioles. The Orioles had won the last three pennants, and six members of that team would eventually be elected to the Baseball Hall of Fame. They were notorious for rugged play.

Wagner (front row, third from left) with his team- mates on the 1898 Louisville team. The maga- zine Sporting Life *offered the opinion that "Wagner won't set the league afire as a third baseman," but he starred at the hot corner in addition to batting a solid .305 during his first full season.*

"My first time up," Wagner recalled, "I got a single. The next time I hit a good one. I might have made a triple but Jack Doyle gave me the hip at first base, Ol' Hughie Jennings chased me wide around second, and John McGraw blocked me off at third and knocked the wind outa me putting the ball in my belly."

Manager Fred Clarke was outraged. "Listen, you iron-headed Dutchman," he told the rookie. "Those are the Orioles. That's their kind of game, that rough stuff. Are you going to stand there and take it?"

Wagner, a peace-loving man by nature, got the message. If that was how they played in the big leagues, he would do the same. Later in the game he walloped another ball deep into center field. This time, he dumped Doyle at first, left Jennings sprawling in the dirt on second, and

trampled all over McGraw at third. "That's the way to play ball, young feller!" Clarke shouted happily. From that day on, Wagner owned the respect of the Orioles. And for the rest of his life, McGraw said that Wagner was the greatest ballplayer he had ever seen.

Wagner finished out the season in Louisville and wound up with a .344 batting average. As he had done at Paterson, he played almost everywhere except shortstop. But wherever Wagner played in the field, he was always a threat at the plate. He batted .305 in 1898 and .359 in 1899.

In the history of baseball, except for Wagner himself, who won the title eight times, there have been very few batting champions who played shortstop. It has been argued that short-stops use up so much energy on defense that they have little left for offense. If this theory is true, it is difficult to imagine what feats Wagner might have accomplished had he stayed in the outfield.

With his easy, loping stride, Wagner covered a wide expanse of ground. But it was his throwing arm that made him such a feared outfielder. Even after he had been switched to shortstop by Fred Clarke, the two would swap positions in crucial situations. The manager, who was also the team's left fielder, would tell Wagner, "We might need a throw to the plate and you've got a better arm than I have." More than once Wagner saved a game by throwing a runner out at the plate. It was still too early in Wagner's major league career for his versatility to be fully appreciated. But opposing teams would soon learn—to their chagrin—that Honus Wagner could beat them in every phase of the game.

3

COMING HOME

Wagner toward the beginning of his career with the Pittsburgh Pirates. Soon after he was transferred to the Pirates, he told manager Fred Clarke, "I aim to stay a Pirate all my life"—and despite a lucrative offer to jump to the newly formed American League, he did just that.

At the end of the 1899 season, the National League was cut down from 12 to 8 teams: New York, Brooklyn, Boston, and Philadelphia in the East; Chicago, Cincinnati, St. Louis, and Pittsburgh in the West. These same clubs would make up the league for the next 52 seasons. Louisville was not one of them.

Barney Dreyfuss, president of the Louisville club, bought a half interest in the Pittsburgh Pirates and took Clarke, Wagner, and 13 others with him to Pittsburgh. The three men—Wagner, Clarke, and Dreyfuss—would be together for the next 16 years and win the National League pennant four times.

Wagner could not have been happier with the change. Now he could live at home all year and be close to his family and friends. As a boy he had walked seven miles each way to see Pittsburgh play on the site of what is now Three Rivers Stadium. He could hardly wait to play there himself. "I aim to stay a Pirate all my life," Wagner told Clarke. "It's where I belong."

A new century began as Wagner joined the

Pirates. It was a time for change and growth. In 1900 there were slightly more than 76 million people living in the United States, and most made their homes in small towns or lived on farms. Pittsburgh, with a population of 322,000, was considered a sizable city.

Nineteen hundred was also the year that baseball began to develop a second major league. When the National League cut back to eight teams, Ban Johnson, president of the Western League, saw an excellent business opportunity. In 1901, he changed the name of the Western League to the American League and claimed major league status for his creation.

Johnson needed some genuine stars for his new league. And by 1901, there was no bigger star than Honus Wagner. The previous year, the Pirates had finished just three games behind the Brooklyn Dodgers, but Wagner was second to none: he won his first batting championship with a .381 average. Only the smooth-fielding second baseman of the Philadelphia Phillies, Napoleon Lajoie, could compare with him. Johnson had already signed the hard-hitting Frenchman to play for the American League's own Philadelphia franchise, the Athletics.

Johnson now wanted to establish a team in New York City, the home of the National League's Giants, and he wanted to build the team around Honus Wagner. Johnson sent his most trusted representative, Clark Griffith, to tempt Wagner. Griffith, known as the Old Fox, showed Wagner more money than he would ever see in one place in his life when he coolly dropped 20 $1,000 bills on a table. They were there for the taking, but Wagner did not even touch them. Money was never his first concern. Where he played and who his teammates were counted a lot more.

When the 1901 season began, Wagner happily put on his Pirates uniform and began collecting his $5,000 salary. Certainly the Pirates got a bargain, for Wagner played wherever he was needed—sometimes at third base or the outfield, sometimes at shortstop. But he was always the cleanup man in the batting order. Although he did not repeat as batting champion, despite a .361 average, he did lead the league with 120 RBIs. The Flying Dutchman, as he now came to be known, also won his first stolen-base crown with 49. He would win that title four more times over the next eight seasons.

Wagner was deceptively fast. He could run 100 yards, baggy pants flapping, in 10 seconds. He ran like a runaway freight train, careering around the bases on his bowlegs. Wagner lacked the graceful stride of an Olympic sprinter; he simply flattened anyone careless enough to get in his way. He was especially fond of stealing home and managed to accomplish this difficult feat 14 times during his career. On several occasions—most notably the 1909 World Series—he did so after having first stolen second and third.

In 1902, Wagner lost the batting title to a teammate, outfielder Ginger Beaumont, whose batting average of .357 bettered Wagner's .329. A squat, heavyset redhead, Beaumont led the league in base hits for the next three years and regularly scored over 100 runs. More often than not, Beaumont was driven home by the Flying Dutchman. In the 1902 season Wagner again outscored everyone in the league, including

Hall of Famer Fred Clarke spent 19 of his 21 seasons in the major leagues as a player manager. A lifetime .315 hitter, Clarke made the shift from Louisville to Pittsburgh along with Wagner in 1900, and the two immortals played together until Clarke's retirement in 1915.

The revamped Pirates were the toast of Pittsburgh in 1900, when Wagner and 13 of his Louisville teammates joined the club. Wagner quickly won the hearts of the hometown fans, hitting at a .381 clip and winning the first of his record eight batting titles.

Beaumont, tallying 105 runs. He also repeated as RBI leader with 91 and was number one in stolen bases with 42.

Although Wagner would eventually rank fifth in career doubles and third in triples, his home run totals do not seem very impressive by today's standards. This is because he played his entire career in the so-called dead ball era.

It may seem strange to baseball fans today,

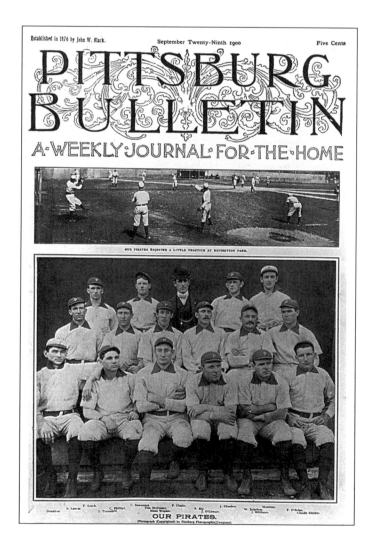

but before Babe Ruth emerged as a crowd-pleasing slugger in the early 1920s, ballplayers did not try to hit home runs. The composition of the ball was such that it did not carry well, and most early ballfields had generous outfield dimensions that put the fences out of reach. The prevailing strategy was to play for one run at a time: singles, doubles, the hit-and-run, bunting, and base stealing were the marrow of the game. As a result, Wagner's highest home run total for a season was 10 in 1908—the league leader that year, Tim Jordan of Brooklyn, hit 12.

The Pittsburgh Pirates of the early 1900s excelled at the basics of the game and became one of the greatest teams of all time. In addition to Ginger Beaumont, Tommy Leach (the best third baseman of his day), and manager Fred Clarke (a lifetime .315 hitter), they had great pitchers. Wagner's good friend Deacon Phillippe, who won 20 games five years in a row, was one of them. Another, until he finally surrendered to the temptations of the American League, was Jack Chesbro, who had led the Pirates to pennants in both 1901 and 1902.

But the greatest pitcher to switch from the National League to the new American League was Denton True "Cy" Young, who jumped to the Boston club in 1901. The pitcher for whom baseball's greatest pitching honor, the Cy Young Award, is named ended up winning 511 major league games, the most ever. A confrontation between Young and Wagner—baseball's best pitcher versus the game's best all-around player—came in 1903 when the National League finally agreed to have its top team meet the American League champions for a world championship series.

THE FIRST WORLD SERIES

Cy Young, leading the new American League in victories for the third straight season, pitched the Boston Pilgrims (later named the Red Sox) to a runaway pennant in 1903. Boston had three 20-game winners: Young with 28, Bill Dinneen with 21, and Long Tom Hughes with 20.

Pittsburgh was not as strong in pitching as Boston. Although Deacon Phillippe was at the top of his form, the Pirates' next-best hurler, Sam Leever, had hurt his shoulder in a skeet-shooting contest, and their third-best starter, Ed Doheny, was hospitalized with emotional problems. As things turned out, pitching depth would be less critical than expected, even though the first World Series was scheduled to be a best-of-nine-games contest. Because of off days for train travel between Boston and Pittsburgh, the prohibition against playing games on Sundays, and torrents of rain, the Series, which began October 1, did not end until October 13. There were ample off days for the

Denton True "Cy" Young, baseball's all-time leader in mound victories with 511, faced off against Wagner and the Pirates in the first World Series in 1903. With Young and Bill Dinneen leading the way, the Boston Pilgrims captured the world championship; Wagner batted only .214 and made several errors in the field.

pitchers to rest, and the teams could recycle their starters with ease.

Wagner had put together another great season in 1903. He not only led the National League in batting (.355) and triples (19) but also managed to steal 46 bases even though a late-season leg injury kept him out of 21 games.

Still ailing, Wagner limped into the Series opener in Boston. But it was the hometown fans who were soon hurting as the Pirates looted Cy Young for four runs in the first inning. In his first at-bat, Wagner singled to drive in a run and then stole second base. Deacon Phillippe shut out Boston for the first six innings, and the Pirates triumphed, 7–3.

The Pilgrims won handily the following day. In the first inning they took advantage of Sam Leever's sore shoulder and scored twice before rookie Bucky Veil took over in the second. Veil then held Boston in check, but the damage had already been done. Bill Dinneen allowed only three hits and earned the 3–1 victory.

Manager Fred Clarke risked sending Deacon Phillippe back to start Game 3 with only one day's rest against Boston's Long Tom Hughes. Again the Pirates got off to a quick start, knocking Hughes out of the box in the third inning. Cy Young, after hitting Wagner, the first batter he faced in relief, kept Pittsburgh from scoring any more, but Boston again lost to the Deacon. Wagner had a double and scored a run in the Pirates' 4–2 win.

On Sunday the teams traveled from Boston to Pittsburgh, where steady rains kept them idle until Wednesday. By then Phillippe was rested enough to start Game 4. Although he won again, 5–4, he weakened in the ninth inning and allowed Boston to score three times. It was clear that the Pirates could not expect Phillippe to win all of the five games they needed.

The next day, with Pittsburgh leading the Series three games to one, Clarke sent veteran Roaring Bill Kennedy to the mound against Cy Young. Kennedy, four times a 20-game winner in the 1890s with Brooklyn, was a colorful character from Bellaire, Ohio. Also known as Brickyard, he had won nine games for Pittsburgh during the regular season. Trainloads of his friends arrived to see him pitch on his 35th birthday.

Roaring Bill got off to a rocky start in the first inning, but Wagner came to his rescue: he threw Boston manager Jimmy Collins out at the plate after Collins had tripled, and Kennedy worked out of a bases-loaded jam. Through the first five innings the immortal Cy Young and the now-forgotten Roaring Bill Kennedy dueled. In the third inning Kennedy even hit a double, and in the fifth he hit a line drive back through the box that Young just managed to handle.

The sixth inning became a nightmare for Wagner. He began by nearly colliding with Fred Clarke, who dropped a fly ball for an error. Two plays later, Wagner dropped a throw on a force play at third, and the bases were loaded. After the unnerved Kennedy walked in a run, Wagner made his second error of the inning. He threw to second with no one covering the base. Before the inning ended, the Pilgrims had scored six unearned runs.

Boston resumed its assault in the next inning, this time scoring four times. Meanwhile, Young had limited Pittsburgh to three hits, and he did not give up a run until the eighth inning, when the Pirates scored twice. The final score was 11–2.

A rare photograph of Boston's Huntington Avenue Baseball Grounds, taken before one of the games of the 1903 World Series. Scheduled to go nine games, the Series was over in eight, as Boston's superior pitching held the Pittsburgh batters in check.

Bill Dinneen started Game 6 against Sam Leever the next day. Although Wagner made another throwing error and went hitless, the Pirates won, 6–3. The Series was tied at three games apiece.

The seventh game was played in Pittsburgh with both starting pitchers from the opening game once more on the mound. This time, however, Young was easily the better of the two. Phillippe went the distance but lost, 7–3. Wagner made still another throwing error and remained hitless.

The teams boarded the train to Boston to finish the first World Series. The Pilgrims needed one more win to clinch the championship. With Bill Dinneen pitching a shutout, they got it. This time, Wagner got one hit and one stolen base. However, he made another wild throw for his sixth error. Worse, he struck out to end the game.

Despite his poor finish in the first World Series ever played, Wagner could take solace in his fine regular season and in the prospect of a fall season hunting rabbits and deer. He would fish, too, as long as he could row a boat out on a lake. And when the lake froze, he would cut a hole in the ice and go right on fishing.

Among ballplayers or old friends, Honus Wagner was an amiable companion. With strangers he was shy and polite. He hated to wear a necktie, and during the off season he avoided parties and formal dinners. In his later years he became a popular speaker on the banquet circuit, often wearing a tuxedo, but as a young player he guarded his privacy closely.

Wagner was adamant about staying in shape year-round, and his love of competition did not diminish during the off season. Fortunately for him, a new game called basketball came into vogue during the early 1900s. The Honus Wagner All-Star Basketball Team played a busy schedule after the 1903 baseball season ended. Wagner was, of course, the team's best player. His long arms were just right for whipping the ball downcourt or snaking it away from an opponent trying to dribble past him. Though early basketball was an extremely low-scoring game, Wagner was the best shooter on the team. One year his All-Stars captured the Western Pennsylvania and Ohio Championship, winning a playoff game by 5–4.

Finally, it was time for baseball again. The Pittsburgh Pirates prepared for 1904 at their usual spring-training site, Hot Springs, Arkansas. Teams went there so players could drink the mineral waters and soak in the hot baths. The Pirates had won the last three National League pennants and confidently expected 1904 to bring yet another championship. After all, they had the best player in the league to lead them to it.

5

THE DUTCHMAN FLIES HIGH

Although Wagner had little formal schooling, his natural intelligence and keen concentration made him one of baseball's most consistent fielders. Pirates executive William Locke once remarked, "I have watched Wagner for many years, and in all that time I have never seen him make a mistake."

Even though baseball players did not wear numbers on their uniforms in Wagner's day, there was never a problem recognizing the Pirates shortstop. With his barrel chest, bowlegs, immensely long arms, and hamlike hands, he resembled no one else in the game. Those hands were like shovels, a great asset in the days when fielders' gloves were small and thinly padded. When Wagner fielded a ground ball he would simply scoop it up along with any pebbles, stones, and loose dirt that happened to be lying around and sling the ball across the diamond with debris trailing it like the tail of a comet. In self-defense, first baseman Kitty Bransfield would help the grounds keeper smooth out the infield around shortstop before each game.

The uniqueness of a great player's talent is often best expressed by other players, who truly understand the difficulty of the game. Tommy Leach, a brilliant third baseman who joined the Louisville club when Wagner was still playing the hot corner, remembered his first sight of the

35

Dutchman: "Well, this big Louisville third base-man jumped over after it [a line drive] like he was on steel springs, slapped it down with his bare hand, scrambled after it at least ten feet, and fired a bullet over to first base. I'm sitting on the bench and my eyes are popping out. So I poked the guy sitting next to me and asked him who the devil that big fellow was on third base. 'Why, that's Wagner,' he says. 'He's the best third baseman in the league.' " When Wagner shifted positions to make room for Leach at third, he starred at first base and in the outfield before settling in as the league's best shortstop.

From 1901 through 1913, three teams won all the National League pennants: the Pittsburgh Pirates, Chicago Cubs, and New York Giants. Pittsburgh won the first three, but then the other teams took over. Still, every year Wagner made Pittsburgh a close contender. The Pirates were always in the first division, mostly finishing second or third. The Cubs built their teams around a Hall of Fame double-play trio—Joe Tinker, Johnny Evers, and Frank Chance—and a strong pitching staff led by Mordecai "Three Finger" Brown. In 1902, the Giants helm had been taken over by the pugnacious John McGraw, who reversed a trend by jumping from the newly formed American League to begin a despotic and highly successful 30-year reign as New York's manager.

In 1904, McGraw's Giants beat out the Pirates and all other National League teams for the first of 11 pennants they would win. Although the Pirates dropped to fourth place that year, Wagner was still the league's domi-nant player. He repeated as batting champion

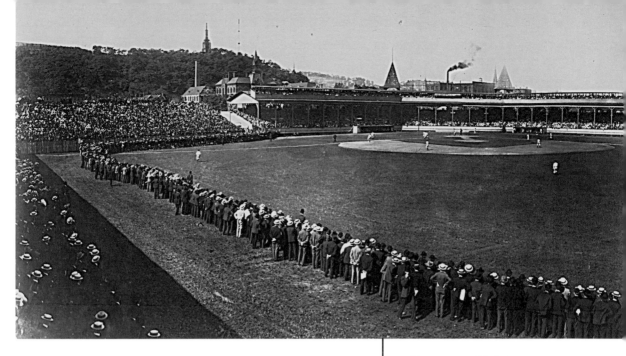

Exposition Park in Pittsburgh, during a 1904 Pirates-Giants game. The outfield dimensions of the old ballparks were so vast that overflow crowds could be accommodated on the playing field; as a result, home runs were rare occurrences—in 1904, Brooklyn's Harry Lumley led the league with nine.

with a .349 average, 20 points higher than his closest rival. He was first in slugging average, total bases, and doubles as well. To top it all off, he repeated as stolen base champion with 53. Wagner also finished second in triples and runs scored, third in hits, and a close fourth in RBIs (75 to the leader's 80).

In 1905 the Giants once again took the National League pennant, with Christy Mathewson a 30-game winner for the third straight year. Pittsburgh moved up to second place, but it was also a runner-up season for Wagner. He lost his batting crown to Cincinnati outfielder Cy Seymour, who rapped out 219 hits to Wagner's 199. Wagner was second to Seymour in slugging average too (.559 to .505), and third in total bases (277), base hits (199), and doubles (32). The Flying Dutchman almost salvaged his stolen-base title but, with 57, finished 2 behind Billy Maloney and Art Devlin, who tied for first place.

Christy Mathewson, one of baseball's finest all-time pitchers, won 20 or more games 13 times during his big league career. However, the great Matty was no puzzle to Wagner, who enjoyed a lifetime .324 average against the Giants hurler.

No one came close to the Chicago Cubs in 1906. They won 116 games, more than any team before or since. It was a great season for Tinker, Evers, and Chance, but Pittsburgh made the most double plays, with Wagner starting most of them. Wagner got back his batting title, hitting .339, and led the league in total bases. He also tied for the lead in runs scored, racked up the most doubles, and just missed making the most hits by one.

In 1907, Wagner's .350 average was good for his fifth batting championship, and he regained his stolen-base title with a personal best of 61. He also led in doubles (38), total bases (264), and slugging percentage (.513), was 2 behind in triples (14), and second both in RBIs (82) and hits (180). Once again, however, he would have to read about the World Series in the Pittsburgh newspapers as the Cubs beat out the Pirates by 17 games for the National League pennant and swept Ty Cobb and his Detroit Tigers in the Series. Then Wagner oiled up his guns, whistled to his dogs, and went hunting. Out in the woods, he considered his retirement.

Wagner was about to turn 34. Although he had played like a young colt the year before, his powerful legs were hurting. He was finally feeling the full effect of the dampness in the coal mines where he had worked as a boy. Rheumatism in his shoulder made throwing painful. Taking stock of his situation, he knew that he was financially secure. The frugal Wagner had saved much of his salary, and he owned the house where he lived with his parents.

During the winter, Wagner met with Pittsburgh owner Barney Dreyfuss, as he did every year, to discuss his contract. Legend would have it that Wagner was naive about money matters and took whatever was offered him. Certainly he was not a mercenary man; he had turned down $20,000 out of loyalty to the Pirates and the National League. He also refused the easy money of vaudeville appearances. Ty Cobb and Napoleon Lajoie, who toured the theaters between seasons, told Wagner he could make $1,000 a week just by appearing onstage with them, but Wagner was not interested. "Ahhh, you know I'm no actor," he replied.

But by 1908 Wagner knew his worth as a player, and he had no intention of punishing his 34-year-old body unless Dreyfuss made it worth his while. Wagner demanded a $10,000 contract, a figure that Dreyfuss considered outrageous. In those days, a player was effectively the property of the club that originally signed him. The only leverage Wagner had was to refuse to play. He told Dreyfuss that if he did not get his $10,000 he would quit baseball and go into the garage business.

Dreyfuss was equally adamant, and when spring training rolled around in 1908, Wagner was home in Pittsburgh. When the season began in April, Dreyfuss realized that Wagner was not bluffing. The Pirates owner finally gave his star player a contract for $10,000, and Wagner rejoined the Pirates for a series with the Cincinnati Reds. As it turned out, $10,000 was the highest salary Wagner would ever earn in the majors, even though his magnificent career still had 10 years to go.

6

THE GREATEST EVERYTHING EVER

The 1908 National League season unfolded into one of the most hotly contested and controversial pennant races of all time. The league's three dominant teams, the Giants, Cubs, and Pirates, took turns in first place all season. The Cubs and the Giants ended in a tie, and the Cubs won the pennant by defeating the Giants in a playoff game, 4–2. The Giants would have won in the regular season, if not for a soon–to–be-legendary baserunning mistake by rookie Fred Merkle that had cost the New Yorkers a late-season win over the Cubs.

The Pirates, who finished just one game out, could have forced a three-way playoff, if not for an umpire's decision that cost them a game in Philadelphia: what appeared to be a game-winning Pittsburgh home run was called a foul ball. But that winter a Philadelphia jury awarded damages to a fan who was injured by the ball. The fan's ticket stub was entered into evidence, and the stub showed that the seat was clearly in fair territory. By then, however, it was too late. The Cubs had already won the pennant and had

Wagner was an avid outdoorsman who loved to hunt and fish during the off-season. A bachelor during his playing career, he is shown here with two of his favorite winter companions.

41

beaten the Detroit Tigers in the World Series.

The season that Honus Wagner had been so reluctant to play turned out to be one of his very best. Despite his aches and pains, he played in 151 games. Wagner won his sixth batting title (.354), breaking the record of five set by Big Dan Brouthers in the 19th century, and led in stolen bases once again (53). He also led in runs batted in (109), was first in slugging percentage (.542) and total bases (308), and headed the list in hits (201), doubles (39), and triples (19).

At this point, Wagner's greatness as a player was universally accepted. In the years to come, only one question about him remained: Was he the greatest of all time? Everyone agreed that Wagner was the greatest shortstop in baseball history. But many fans of the game, then and now, have considered him without peer, based on his versatility and his overall excellence. From 1895 to 1913, Wagner never batted below .300, and his lifetime major league batting average was .328. His 252 triples are still a record. He led the league in batting eight times—a record that stands to this day—and in stolen bases five times. He also led all shortstops in fielding average 11 times.

Ed Barrow, who was general manager of the New York Yankees when Babe Ruth was in his heyday, felt that Wagner was even greater than Ruth, as did the legendary umpire Bill Klem and the acknowledged master at evaluating baseball talent, Branch Rickey. Wahoo Sam Crawford, who played for Detroit with Ty Cobb for many seasons, agreed. The Cubs' Joe Tinker also felt that Wagner outperformed Cobb. Tommy Leach summed up the prevailing view of Wagner's all-around dominance: "It also turned out that while Honus was the best third baseman in the

league, he was also the best first baseman, the best second baseman, the best shortstop, and the best outfielder. That was in fielding. And since he led the league in batting eight times between 1900 and 1911, you know that he was the best hitter, too. As well as the best base runner." In other words, Leach concluded in another interview, "Wagner was the greatest *everything* ever."

In the winter of 1909, Wagner signed yet another contract: he could hardly retire after the extraordinary season he had just enjoyed. The 1909 season was to be a wonderful one for Pittsburgh. A brand-new concrete and steel stadium, Forbes Field, opened in the center of the city, next to scenic Schenley Park. Excited fans

Wagner talks baseball with legendary New York Giants manager John McGraw before a 1915 Pirates-Giants game. Known as Little Napoleon, McGraw was not an easy man to impress; but having both played and managed against Wagner, he considered the Dutchman to be the greatest ballplayer he had ever seen.

Wagner takes batting practice at New York's Polo Grounds in 1908. In addition to his record eight batting titles, Wagner smashed 252 triples during his career, a mark that has never been equaled.

packed the stands all year to watch the Pirates finally outdistance the Cubs and the Giants: the team finished with a brilliant 110-42 record and won the pennant by 6½ games.

Once again, Wagner was the Pirates' mainstay. He led the league in slugging average (.489), total bases (242), RBIs (100), and doubles (39). He also won another batting championship with a .339 average—he had now led the National League for four years in a row. The only sign that he really might be slowing down was

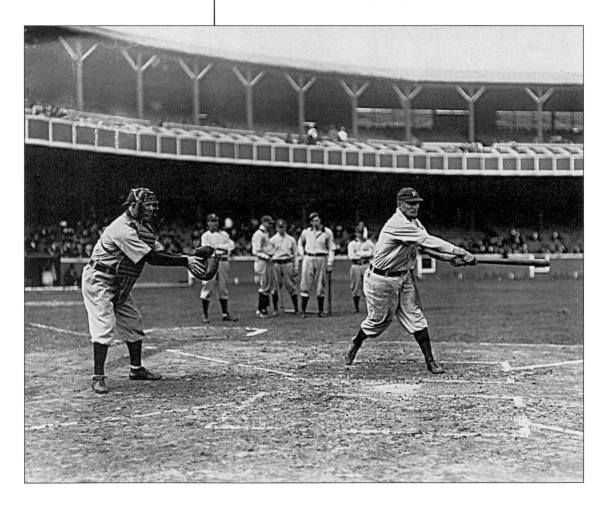

his stolen base total—35. For anyone else, that would have been an excellent effort. But the Flying Dutchman was not just anyone.

At this point in his career, Wagner was accustomed to individual honors; like most great players, what he coveted most was the chance to display his skills in baseball's incomparable showcase, the World Series, and to be part of a world championship team. His previous trip to the Fall Classic, in 1903, had been a disappointment, both for him and the Pirates. In 1909, Wagner had the great satisfaction of seeing his team emerge with the crown. And he had the added pleasure of knowing that he had not only outperformed Ty Cobb—he had also stood up to Cobb's physical challenge and had beaten the Detroit star at his own game.

In those early years of baseball, it was customary for fans who lived in small towns to gather in the general store, put their feet up on the fender of a glowing stove, and rehash the events of the previous season. As the "hot stove league" convened all over the nation during the winter of 1909–10, it is doubtful that there was much disagreement about who was the greatest "everything" in the game of baseball.

From the day he first stepped on a ballfield in his oversize spiked shoes, Honus Wager was a legend in the making. Not only did he pull off sparkling plays, punish the ball, and run the bases better than anyone else, but off the field he was everything a hero should be. A bachelor throughout his years of stardom, he was like a big brother to all the youngsters who trailed him home from the ballpark.

Wagner was a prominent member of the Elks, a leading community service organization. Around his hometown of Mansfield, later renamed Carnegie, he could greet almost everyone by his or her first name. It seemed as if the durable Dutchman would be a hometown hero forever.

However, after the triumphant 1909 World Series, Wagner slipped somewhat. In 1910, as Pittsburgh dropped back to third place, Wagner finished fifth in the batting race, hitting .320, his lowest average in over a decade. He was fifth in RBIs, too. Although he did tie for the most hits, he was not among the leaders in doubles,

In December 1916, when he was 41 years old and approaching his last season as a player, Wagner married Bessie Baine Smith, a Pittsburgh native and the daughter of a former pitcher. This photo of the newlyweds confirms what his friends said of Wagner—that although he hated formal clothes, when he wore them, he wore them well.

triples, or stolen bases. The Dutchman was not running the basepaths as fast as he once had.

The next year, 1911, Wagner collected another batting title, hitting .344. It was the eighth time that he had led the National League, an accomplishment that remains unmatched. However, there was not to be a ninth batting crown.

Each winter, Wagner would think about retirement, and each spring he would decide to help his team as much as he could for another season. By 1914, however, the Pirates were beyond his help. They had dropped out of the first division. And that same year, Wagner hit below .300 for the first time in his major league career.

Wagner was still as durable as ever, playing 150 games in 1914 and 151 games in 1915. His instinct for where to play the hitters had not declined, and his shovel-like hands were as sure as ever. He led the league's shortstops in fielding average his last two full seasons at the position. And although Wagner had become a mere mortal as a batter, in 1914 he knocked out his 3,000th hit. Only Cap Anson, who retired with 3,041 hits over 22 seasons played during the 19th century, had ever reached the 3,000-hit mark. Coincidentally, Anson got his 3,000th big league hit in 1897, the year Wagner began his own career in the majors.

Wagner passed Anson's career total in 1915. In the same year, Napoleon Lajoie, who had followed Wagner into the very exclusive 3,000-hit club in 1914, also broke Anson's mark. By the end of the 1916 season, Lajoie had upped his total to 3,251, but Wagner was still ahead with 3,369. Lajoie then conceded the record and retired. Wagner had now lost a big incentive to keep playing, but he decided to come back for one more season.

In one important way, Wagner's life was just beginning. On December 30, 1916, at the age of 42, Wagner finally got married. His bride was a young woman from Pittsburgh, Bessie Baine Smith, who had excellent baseball genes. "Her father was a mighty fine pitcher," Wagner told his fans. "As a kid, I used to watch him play. Had one of the sweetest curve balls I ever saw in my life." Presumably he would have married Smith anyway, but her father's curveball was an added incentive.

The following spring Wagner was back with the Pirates, believing that he had one more good year in him. But 1917 was a disaster for him and his teammates.

Jimmy Callahan had succeeded Fred Clarke as the Pittsburgh manager, but he was fired in June as the Pirates struggled. Barney Dreyfuss tried to convince Wagner to take over the helm,

In addition to hunting and fishing, Wagner (back row, center) kept himself busy during the winter by playing the newly invented game of basketball. This photograph shows Hans Wagner's All-Stars during the 1908–9 season.

though the Dutchman insisted over and over that he "wasn't cut out to be a manager." He finally gave in, but only on condition that he would not be saddled with any of the team's business matters. On Wagner's first day as manager, June 30, the Pirates defeated the Cincinnati Reds. But then they promptly lost their next four games, and Wagner decided that he had had enough. His managerial career officially ended on July 5. He agreed to stay on as a player but found that he could no longer cover the ground at shortstop. Mostly he played first base, appearing in only 74 games and batting a disappointing .265. When the Pirates finished dead last, Wagner went home for good.

Wagner was out of the major leagues, but he was not ready to hang up his spikes. He organized the Honus Wagner Baseball All-Stars and began playing semiprofessional baseball in the Pittsburgh area. In the winter, he kept busy with his All-Star Basketball Team. Wagner played for both teams until it got to be too much for him, and then he quit basketball. He continued to play baseball for a number of years; even though running the bases became harder every year, he could still rap out base hits.

Wagner coached baseball and basketball at Carnegie Tech for several years, and his friends had him appointed sergeant at arms for the Pennsylvania State Legislature. But that was one job he did not enjoy—he had to listen to too many political speeches. During the late 1920s, Wagner and another Pirates star, Pie Traynor, opened a sporting goods store in downtown Pittsburgh, but their timing was bad. The United States soon plunged into a deep economic depression, and the business lost a lot of money.

Wagner, who now had two daughters, Betty and Virginia, struggled to make ends meet until 1933, when the Pirates offered him a job as a coach. He eagerly agreed to don the Pittsburgh uniform again, and baseball was equally glad to have him back.

Everywhere the team played, the Flying Dutchman was given an enthusiastic welcome. In Brooklyn, the home of the Dodgers, there was a motorcade and a huge formal dinner in Wagner's honor. Wagner responded to the attention, and he soon found himself attending a host of public functions on behalf of the ballclub. Having spent his illustrious playing career saying as little as possible and shunning the limelight, Wagner now became one of the stars of the banquet circuit, renowned for his vivid if somewhat improbable stories.

For most of his yarns, Wagner drew upon his many years in baseball or his experiences on hunting trips. One favorite combined both

Among other business ventures, Wagner (second from right) opened a sporting goods store with another Pirates star, Pie Traynor (fourth from right). When the business went under during the Great Depression of the 1930s, a financially strapped Wagner gladly returned to baseball as a Pittsburgh coach.

sources. "I had this retriever who had only one problem," Wagner told his audiences. "He'd fetch something but he wouldn't give it up. One day I had him at the ballpark and he got loose during the game. A friend of mine was on the other team and he knew about my dog. He hit a ground ball just past me and the dog chased after it and brought it back. I tried to wrestle it away from him but he wouldn't let loose. The batter kept running, figuring my dog wouldn't give up the ball. Finally, as the runner went past me, I did the only thing I could. I picked up the dog and threw him to the third baseman. He tagged the runner out with the dog."

Another story concerned Wagner's hobby of keeping pigeons. Supposedly Wagner once bet Fred Clarke that if Clarke took one of Wagner's carrier pigeons back to his ranch in Kansas and released it, the bird would find its way home. Clarke took the bird back to Kansas, but clipped its wings before releasing it, remarking, "Now,

Wagner enjoyed a successful career as a coach for the Pirates for almost two decades. He took a kindly interest in all the team's players and kept them entertained with his tall tales.

let's see you get back home!" But Wagner won the bet because the pigeon did come back five months later—with very sore feet, he explained.

Wagner was an active and enthusiastic coach. He hit grounders for infield practice and made himself useful before the game. And whenever he took a turn in fielding or batting practice, silence came over the field as every ballplayer—both on the Pirates and the opposition—quit whatever he was doing to watch the legendary Dutchman. But as the years went by, the players worried about their coach, who was now in his seventies. When Wagner was hit in the back with a line drive, they finally talked him into staying on the bench.

Unlike many old-timers, Wagner got along wonderfully with the young players. He never compared them to the players of his era, least of all to himself. He always encouraged them, gave them tips on how to improve their play, and listened sympathetically when they told him their problems.

The following incident, while it took place long before Wagner was a coach, illustrates his sensitivity to other players. In one game, a Pittsburgh player struck out with the bases loaded. As the player returned crestfallen to the bench, Wagner approached him and said, "Do you know, I went up to the plate with the bases full once, and it was in World's Series time too. A little hit of mine would have scored the winning run, and do you know, I struck out." The first part of Wagner's statement was true, but instead of striking out as he had diplomatically informed the outfielder, he had hit a ringing drive for extra bases.

IMMORTALITY

In 1936, the leaders of organized baseball agreed that it was time to create the Baseball Hall of Fame, a national shrine honoring the great players of the game. They decided to locate the new institution in the upstate New York hamlet of Cooperstown, where, according to a long-held belief, Abner Doubleday had invented the game of baseball in 1839. The nation's baseball writers were given the task of choosing the first five entrants.

To no one's surprise, Honus Wagner was chosen for the elite group of baseball immortals, along with Babe Ruth, Christy Mathewson, Walter Johnson, and Wagner's old rival, Ty Cobb.

When the Hall of Fame opened on June 12, 1939, Wagner took a rare day off from his coaching duties to attend the induction ceremony. He sat on the platform proudly, sharing the memorable moment with some of baseball's greatest players. Wagner's bronze plaque described him as "the greatest shortstop in baseball history."

Always fond of young people, Wagner shares some of his batting secrets during a 1945 baseball clinic at Philadelphia's Shibe Park.

Wagner coached the Pirates for 18 years, almost as long as he had played for them. He finally retired after the 1951 season, at the age of 77.

Four years later, on April 30, 1955, a massive nine-foot-high statue of Wagner was set in place in Schenley Park, outside the left-field gates at Forbes Field. The statue, by sculptor Frank Vittor, captured the Dutchman in his prime, taking a lusty cut at the ball. It had cost $40,000 to complete and install the statue, but Wagner's friends and admirers felt it was well worth it.

The 81-year-old Wagner, who had been ill for some time, enjoyed the festivities from an open automobile in front of the statue. His once-powerful legs were no longer strong enough to climb the steps to the platform where the honored guests sat. But a smile lit up his pale, gaunt face as he watched his four-year-old granddaughter, Leslie Ann Blair, pull the cord that unveiled the statue. He listened happily while his former teammates and rivals expressed their love for him and gratitude for all he had given his sport. National League President Warren Giles praised Wagner as "probably the greatest player in the game." Wagner's old manager, Fred Clarke, recalled how Wagner was "an outfielder

Wagner poses with other diamond immortals at the 1939 dedication of the Baseball Hall of Fame. Left to right, rear: Wagner, Grover Cleveland Alexander, Tris Speaker, Napoleon Lajoie, George Sisler, and Walter Johnson. Left to right, front: Eddie Collins, Babe Ruth, Connie Mack, and Cy Young.

without equal" before he became a shortstop. Perhaps the greatest honor bestowed upon Wagner that day was Cy Young's presence. At the age of 88, Young had come from his home in Ohio to recall the first World Series in 1903, when he had pitched against Wagner. After all the speeches were over, Wagner's convertible drew slowly away as more than 1,000 fans and family friends said what was to be their last good-bye.

Eight months later, on December 6, 1955, Honus Wagner died in his sleep in his Carnegie, Pennsylvania, home.

In addition to his stature as one of baseball's all-time greats, an even more unusual form of immortality has come to Wagner. The most valuable item of baseball memorabilia is the 1910 Honus Wagner card, which was recently sold for $100,000—more money than Wagner earned in his whole career as a player. Wagner himself had inadvertently raised the card's value years earlier by objecting to its use by a tobacco company.

A local photographer had been paid $10 for the picture, and Wagner, with his typical kindness, was sorry the man would lose his fee. After telling the tobacco company to withdraw the card, he sent the photographer a check, along with a letter that was proudly displayed in the man's shop window for many years. "I don't want you to miss the chance to sell a picture," Wagner wrote, "but I don't want my photograph to help sell cigarettes to kids." As a result of Wagner's action, only a few 1910 Wagner cards went into circulation before they were removed from the cigarette packs. The few that survive have become the rarest of all baseball cards—just as Honus Wagner was the rarest of baseball players.

CHRONOLOGY

1874	Born Johannes Peter Wagner in Mansfield, Pennsylvania, on February 24
1886	Goes to work in coal mines at age 12
1892	Begins semipro career in Allegheny League
1895	Becomes professional ballplayer
1897	Makes major league debut with Louisville in National League on July 19
1900	Joins Pittsburgh Pirates and wins first of eight batting titles with a .381 average
1901	Turns down $20,000 offer to jump to newly formed American League
1903	Plays in the first World Series
1904	Leads National League in batting, slugging, total bases, doubles, and stolen bases
1907	Bats .350, winning his fifth hitting crown; steals 61 bases, his career high
1908	Signs $10,000 contract, his highest in the majors; leads the league in every important offensive category
1909	Wins fourth consecutive batting title; leads Pirates to World Series victory over Detroit Tigers
1916	Marries Bessie Baine Smith on December 30
1917	Plays final season in major leagues
1933	Rejoins Pirates as coach
1936	Elected to Baseball Hall of Fame, in the first group of five immortals
1951	Retires as coach of Pirates at age 77
1955	Dies in Carnegie, Pennsylvania, on December 6

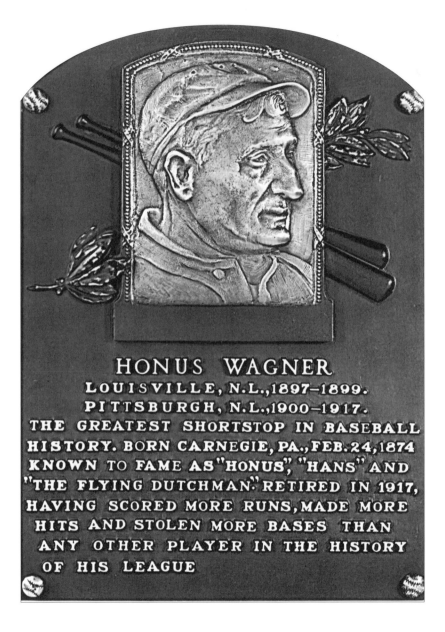

HONUS WAGNER
LOUISVILLE, N.L.,1897-1899.
PITTSBURGH, N.L.,1900-1917.
THE GREATEST SHORTSTOP IN BASEBALL
HISTORY. BORN CARNEGIE, PA., FEB. 24, 1874
KNOWN TO FAME AS "HONUS", "HANS" AND
"THE FLYING DUTCHMAN." RETIRED IN 1917,
HAVING SCORED MORE RUNS, MADE MORE
HITS AND STOLEN MORE BASES THAN
ANY OTHER PLAYER IN THE HISTORY
OF HIS LEAGUE

MAJOR LEAGUE STATISTICS

LOUISVILLE COLONELS, PITTSBURGH PIRATES

YEAR	TEAM	G	AB	R	H	2B	3B	HR	RBI	BA	SB
1897	LOU N	61	241	38	83	17	4	2	39	.344	19
1898		151	591	80	180	31	4	10	105	.305	27
1899		147	571	102	197	47	13	7	113	.345	37
1900	PIT N	135	528	107	201	45	22	4	100	.381	38
1901		141	556	100	196	37	10	6	126	.353	49
1902		137	538	105	177	33	16	3	91	.329	42
1903		129	512	97	182	30	19	5	101	.355	46
1904		132	490	97	171	44	14	4	75	.349	53
1905		147	548	114	199	32	14	6	101	.363	57
1906		142	516	103	175	38	9	2	71	.339	53
1907		142	515	98	180	38	14	6	82	.350	61
1908		151	568	100	201	39	19	10	109	.354	53
1909		137	495	92	168	39	10	5	100	.339	35
1910		150	556	90	178	34	8	4	81	.320	24
1911		130	473	87	158	23	16	9	89	.334	20
1912		145	558	91	181	35	20	7	102	.324	26
1913		114	413	51	124	18	4	3	56	.300	21
1914		150	552	60	139	15	9	1	50	.252	23
1915		151	566	68	155	32	17	6	78	.274	22
1916		123	432	45	124	15	9	1	39	.287	11
1917		74	230	15	61	7	1	0	24	.265	5
Totals		2789	10449	1740	3430	649	252	101	1732	.328	722

World Series

1903		8	27	2	6	1	0	0	3	.222	6
1909		7	24	4	8	2	1	0	6	.333	6
Totals		15	51	6	14	3	1	0	9	.278	12

FURTHER READING

Broeg, Bob. *Super Stars of Baseball.* St. Louis: The Sporting News, 1971.

Carmichael, John P., ed. *My Greatest Day in Baseball.* New York: A. S. Barnes, 1945.

Davis, Mac. *100 Greatest Baseball Heroes.* New York: Grossett & Dunlap, 1974.

Einstein, Charles, ed. *The Third Fireside Book of Baseball.* New York: Simon & Schuster, 1968.

Honig, Donald. *The Donald Honig Reader.* New York: Simon & Schuster, 1988.

Meany, Thomas. *Baseball's Greatest Hitters.* New York: A. S. Barnes, 1950.

———. *Baseball's Greatest Teams—1909 Pirates.* New York: A. S. Barnes, 1949.

Neft, David S., Richard M. Cohen, et al. *The Sports Encyclopedia: Baseball.* New York: St. Martin's, 1993.

Reidenbaugh, Lowell. *Baseball's Hall of Fame: Cooperstown, Where the Legends Live Forever.* New York: Arlington House, 1988.

Sahadi, Lou. *The Pirates.* New York: Times Books, 1980.

Seymour, Harold. *Baseball—The Golden Age.* New York: Oxford University Press, 1971.

Sher, Jack. *Twelve Sport Immortals.* New York: Bartholomew House, 1949.

Starr, Bill. *Clearing the Bases: Baseball Then and Now.* New York: Michael Kesend, 1989.

Wind, Herbert Warren, ed. *The Realm of Sport.* New York: Simon & Schuster, 1966.

INDEX

PICTURE CREDITS

Bettmann: pp. 22, 44, 54, 56; The Carnegie Library of Pittsburgh: pp. 8, 26, 28, 34, 37; Historical Society of Western Pennsylvania: p. 14; National Baseball Library, Cooperstown, NY: pp. 12–13, 18, 20, 25, 30, 32, 38, 40, 43, 46, 49, 51, 52, 58, 60; *The Sporting News:* pp. 2, 11

JACK KAVANAGH, a freelance writer of sports stories, began writing about sports as a high school correspondent for the *Brooklyn Eagle* in the 1930s. He has been a contributing editor to *Sports History,* and his writing has appeared in various magazines, including *Sports Heritage, Vine Line,* and *Diversions.* His work is included in *The Ball Players, Total Baseball,* and other baseball anthologies. Mr. Kavanagh lives in North Kingston, Rhode Island.

JIM MURRAY, veteran sports columnist of the *Los Angeles Times,* is one of America's most acclaimed writers. He has been named "America's Best Sportswriter" by the National Association of Sportscasters and Sportswriters 14 times, was awarded the Red Smith Award, and was twice winner of the National Headliner Award. In addition, he was awarded the J. G. Taylor Spink Award in 1987 for "meritorious contributions to baseball writing." With this award came his 1988 induction into the National Baseball Hall of Fame in Cooperstown, New York. In 1990, Jim Murray was awarded the Pulitzer Prize for Commentary.

EARL WEAVER is the winningest manager in the Baltimore Orioles history by a wide margin. He compiled 1,480 victories in his 17 years at the helm. After managing eight different minor league teams, he was given the chance to lead the Orioles in 1968. Under his leadership the Orioles finished lower than second place in the American League East only four times in 17 years. One of only 12 managers in big league history to have managed in four or more World Series, Earl was named Manager of the Year in 1979. The popular Weaver had his number 5 retired in 1982, joining Brooks Robinson, Frank Robinson, and Jim Palmer, whose numbers were retired previously. Earl Weaver continues his association with the professional baseball scene by writing, broadcasting, and coaching.